This is not an official Barbie book. It is not approved by or connected with Mattel, Inc.

This edition first published in 2025 by Bellwether Media, Inc.

No part of this publication may be reproduced in whole or in part without written permission of the publisher.
For information regarding permission, write to Bellwether Media, Inc., Attention: Permissions Department,
6012 Blue Circle Drive, Minnetonka, MN 55343.

Library of Congress Cataloging-in-Publication Data

LC record for Barbie available at: https://lccn.loc.gov/2024021922

Text copyright © 2025 by Bellwether Media, Inc. BLASTOFF! DISCOVERY and associated logos are trademarks and/or registered trademarks of Bellwether Media, Inc. Bellwether Media is a division of Chrysalis Education Group.

Editor: Betsy Rathburn   Series Designer: Andrea Schneider   Book Designer: Josh Brink

Printed in the United States of America, North Mankato, MN.

TABLE OF CONTENTS

DREAM DOLLS	4
BARBIE'S BEGINNINGS	6
GROWTH AND CHANGE	20
BETTER WITH BARBIE	26
BARBIE FANS	28
GLOSSARY	30
TO LEARN MORE	31
INDEX	32

DREAM DOLLS

A girl pulls out her favorite Barbie dolls. One is a scientist. The other is a snowboarder. They come with many clothes and **accessories**. The girl decides her dolls are going on a trip. She places them into her Barbie Dreamplane. They can go anywhere!

The girl gets out more Barbies. Each one has a special look or a cool career. They have different hairstyles and outfits. It is fun to mix and match them! Later, the girl turns on a Barbie movie. She settles in for a fun night with her favorite toys!

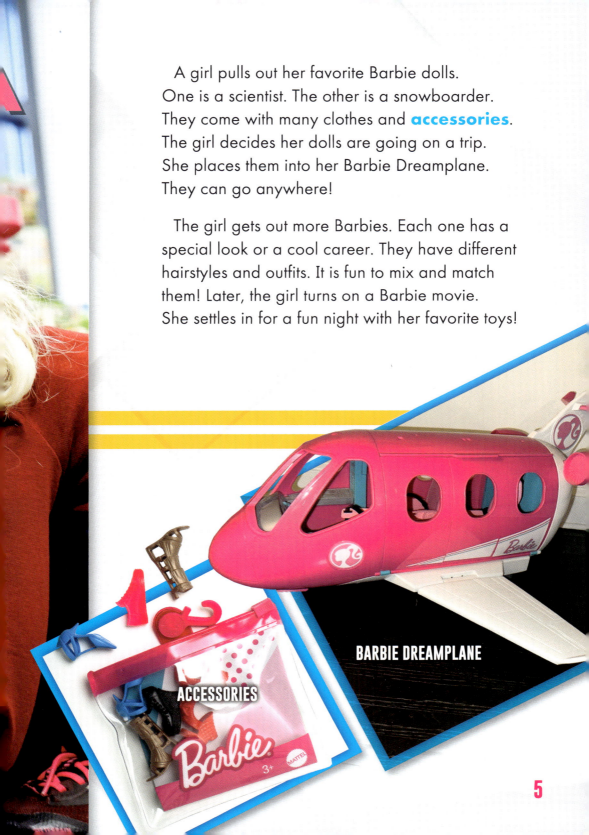

BARBIE DREAMPLANE

ACCESSORIES

BARBIE'S BEGINNINGS

Barbie is the world's most popular fashion doll! The **brand** is owned by the toy company Mattel. Mattel's **headquarters** is in El Segundo, California. The brand has many lines that include a wide variety of dolls. The dolls have different careers, looks, and more.

The Barbie brand includes many accessories. Fans can collect houses, cars, and extra outfits. Barbie media also excites fans. People can read Barbie books, watch Barbie movies, and even play Barbie video games. This brand is full of fun!

TALL DOLL
A standard Barbie doll is 11.5 inches (29 centimeters) tall.

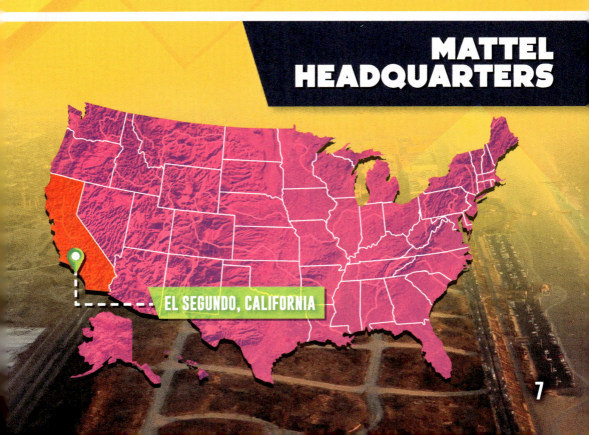

MATTEL HEADQUARTERS

EL SEGUNDO, CALIFORNIA

7

Mattel began in California in 1945. Ruth Handler, her husband Elliot, and their partner Harold Matson **founded** the company. It first sold picture frames and dollhouse furniture. Later, it moved to toys.

THREE-DOLLAR DOLL

In 1959, a Barbie doll cost $3. Today, an original doll in perfect condition can sell for over $27,000!

RUTH HANDLER

BORN November 4, 1916, in Denver, Colorado

DIED April 27, 2002

ROLE Cofounder of Mattel

ACCOMPLISHMENTS

Invented the Barbie doll and helped it become the world's most popular fashion doll

1959 BARBIE DOLL

RUTH AND ELLIOT HANDLER

In the 1950s, baby dolls were the most popular dolls. But Ruth and Elliot's daughter, Barbara, enjoyed paper dolls. They inspired Ruth to make a new kind of doll, one that would help girls imagine themselves as adults. Ruth created the Barbie doll. It **debuted** in 1959. Many doubted it would sell well. But **advertisements** during children's TV shows helped Mattel sell more than 300,000 dolls in Barbie's first year!

9

The Barbie brand grew quickly. In 1960, Barbie got her first career. Mattel released a fashion designer Barbie. The next year, a Barbie nurse, flight attendant, and ballerina came out. More careers soon followed.

EARLY BARBIE CAREERS

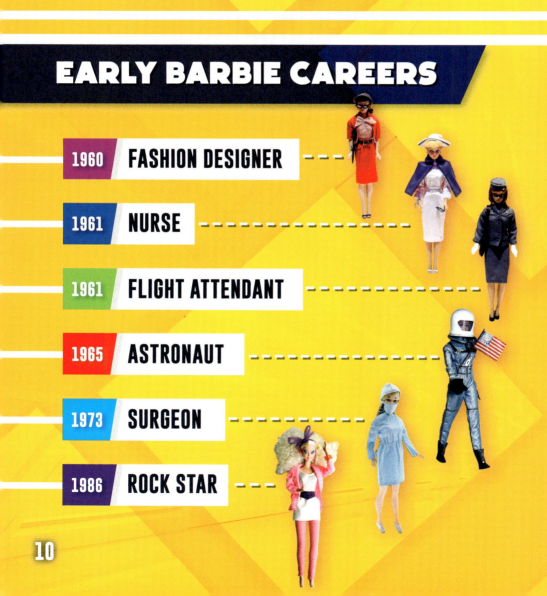

1960	FASHION DESIGNER
1961	NURSE
1961	FLIGHT ATTENDANT
1965	ASTRONAUT
1973	SURGEON
1986	ROCK STAR

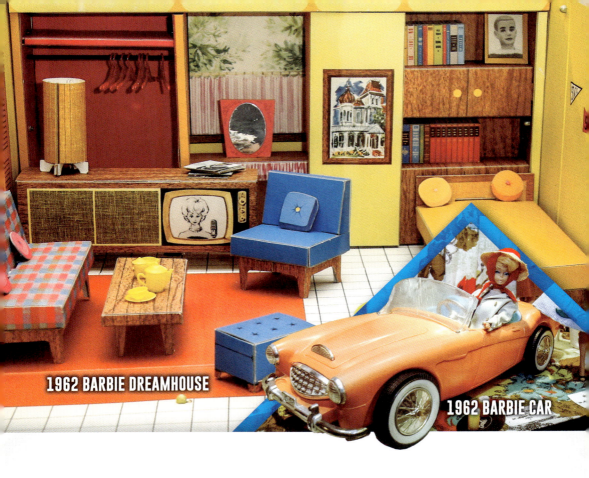

1962 BARBIE DREAMHOUSE

1962 BARBIE CAR

In 1962, Mattel gave Barbie a place to live. The first Barbie Dreamhouse was released! The cardboard house had furniture, wall art, and a closet for Barbie's outfits. Mattel launched a Barbie car, too. The car had an open top and came in many colors. Barbie fit behind the wheel!

MANY JOBS

Since 1959, Barbie has held more than 250 different careers.

11

The 1960s also brought new friends for Barbie. In 1961, Ken was released. Midge was released in 1963 as Barbie's best friend. Allan and Skipper were released in 1964. Allan was Ken's friend. Skipper was Barbie's younger sister.

These releases helped the Barbie brand grow. But the line of dolls was not **diverse**. Barbie and friends were all white. In 1968, that began to change. The Christie doll was released as Barbie's friend. She is considered the brand's first Black doll.

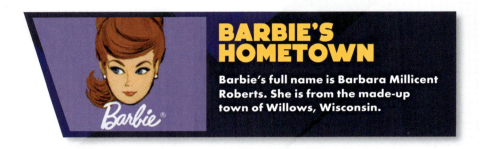

BARBIE'S HOMETOWN

Barbie's full name is Barbara Millicent Roberts. She is from the made-up town of Willows, Wisconsin.

CHRISTIE

13

The Barbie brand continued to grow in the 1970s. In 1971, Malibu Barbie was released. She had an open smile and straight blonde hair. Her eyes looked forward instead of to the side. People loved the new look! More dolls in the Malibu line followed.

DOLLS OF THE WORLD

The Dolls of the World line includes Barbies from different countries around the world. The first dolls in the line were from Italy, France, and England.

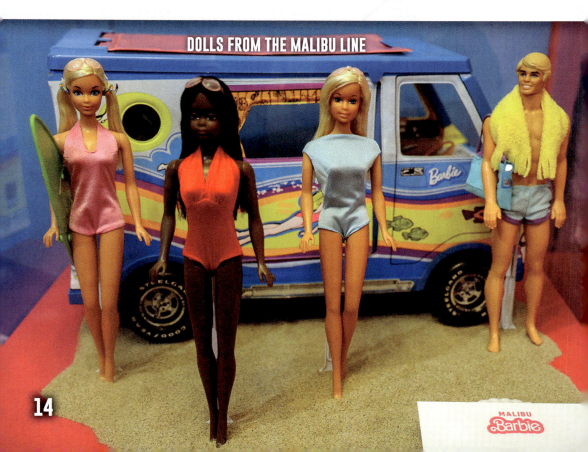

DOLLS FROM THE MALIBU LINE

14

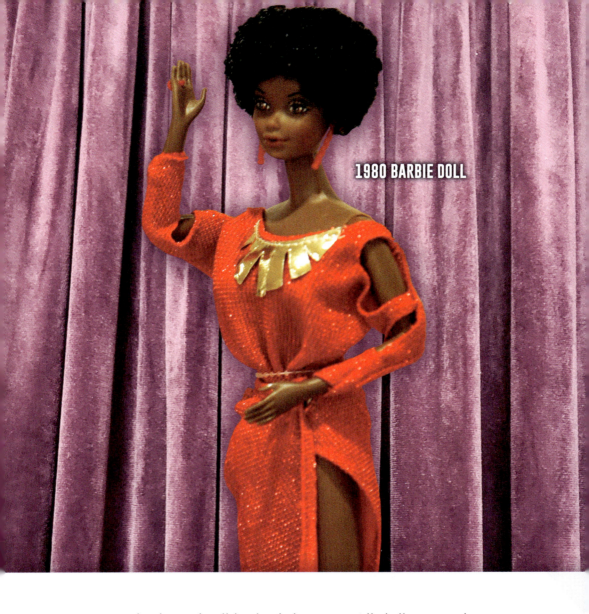

1980 BARBIE DOLL

But the brand still lacked diversity. All dolls named Barbie were white. Many wanted Mattel to release more dolls with different features and more skin tones. In 1980, Mattel released new dolls **marketed** as Black and Hispanic. They were the first diverse dolls named Barbie. More kids could play with a Barbie that looked like them!

More growth came in the 1980s. In 1985, Mattel launched the We Girls Can Do Anything **campaign**. It was meant to inspire girls to dream big, just like Barbie!

MUSIC MOVIE
Barbie and the Rockers dolls starred in a 1987 TV movie. It is called *Barbie and the Rockers: Out of This World.*

Mattel also released many special Barbie dolls in the 1980s. Horse Lovin' Barbie and her friends rode horses. Dream Glow Barbie wore clothes that glowed in the dark. Dolls in the 1986 Barbie and the Rockers line were in a band. Barbie sales grew along with its new lines. In 1988, the brand sold more than 20 million dolls!

HORSE LOVIN' BARBIE

BARBIE AND THE ROCKERS DOLLS

By the 1990s, Mattel was releasing special Barbies each year. It introduced Totally Hair Barbie in 1992. The doll's long hair reached its feet. It became the best-selling Barbie of all time! Another popular release that year was a Barbie running for President of the United States.

NEW FRIENDS

In 1999, Mattel started the Generation Girl line of Barbies. It included Barbie and five other dolls with different names and personalities.

TOTALLY HAIR BARBIE

SHARE A SMILE BECKY

18

BARBIE TIMELINE

1959 — The first Barbie doll debuts

1961 — The first Barbie with a career is released

1988 — Mattel sells 20 million Barbie dolls over the year

1997 — Share a Smile Becky is released

2019 — The Barbie Dream Gap Project begins

1961 — The first Ken doll debuts

1968 — Mattel introduces Christie, considered the brand's first Black doll

1992 — A Barbie doll running for U.S. president is released

2016 — Barbie releases the Fashionistas line

2023 — The live-action movie *Barbie* is released

In 1997, Mattel debuted Share a Smile Becky, a doll that used a wheelchair. This was an effort to make Barbie more **inclusive**. But many felt this was not enough. They were disappointed that her wheelchair did not fit in the Barbie Dreamhouse. People continued to call for more diversity.

19

GROWTH AND CHANGE

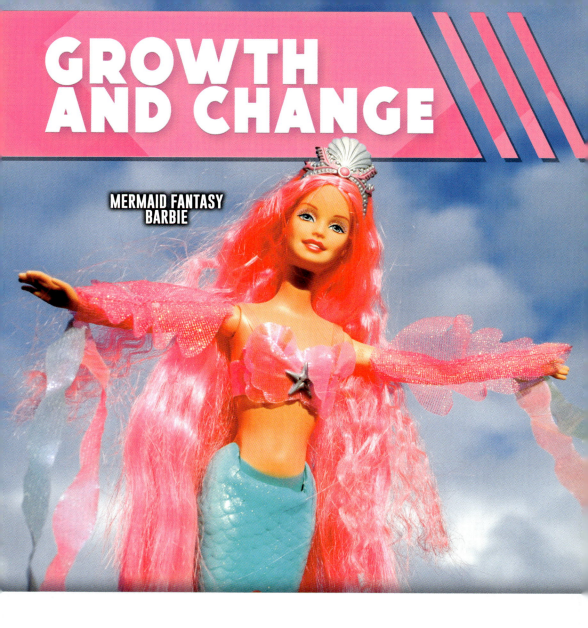

MERMAID FANTASY BARBIE

Barbie's popularity continued into the 2000s. In 2002, Jewel Girl Barbie came out. It included gems to attach to Barbie's hair and clothes. In 2003, Mermaid Fantasy Barbie debuted. Instead of legs, the doll had sparkly tail fins!

Beyond dolls, people could enjoy Barbie in other ways. Many **animated** Barbie movies started coming out in the 2000s. The first was *Barbie in the Nutcracker*. It released in 2001. More than a dozen Barbie movies followed. Barbie video games became popular in the 2000s, too. Fans followed Barbie as she did secret missions, competed in sports, and more!

FIRST VIDEO GAME
The first Barbie video game came out in 1984. It was played on a computer called the Commodore 64.

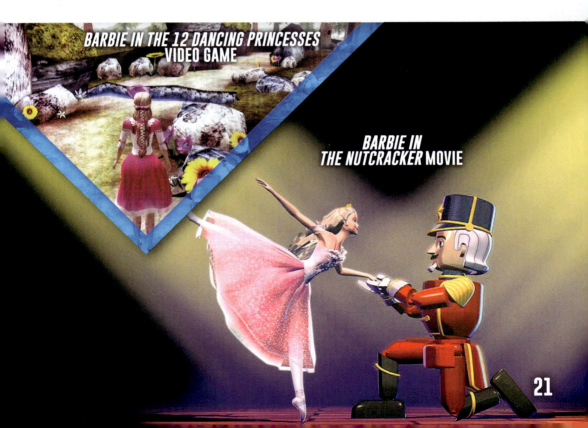

BARBIE IN THE 12 DANCING PRINCESSES VIDEO GAME

BARBIE IN THE NUTCRACKER MOVIE

By 2009, more than 1 billion Barbies had sold. Then in the 2010s, Barbie sales began to slow. Electronic toys were growing more popular. People were also buying more diverse dolls from other brands. The Barbie brand was in trouble.

In response, Mattel debuted the Fashionistas line in 2016. Barbies in this line have varying body types, skin tones, abilities, and hairstyles. Barbie sales rose again. The Fashionistas line continued adding more diverse dolls. Some have **prosthetic** limbs or hearing aids. In 2023, the first Barbie with **Down syndrome** was released.

2016 FASHIONISTAS LINE

BARBIE SALES

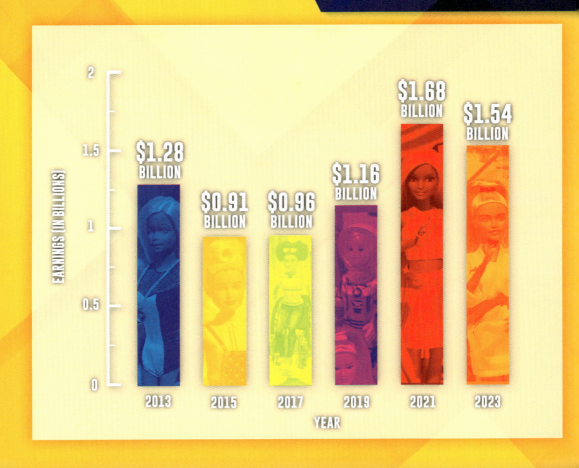

FASHION FAVORITES

The Fashionistas line has 9 different body types and 35 different skin tones!

BARBIE MOVIE

The 2020s have brought even more to the Barbie brand. Barbie got new careers, including sports reporter and music producer. In 2023, the first President Barbie was released. It was based on a character from *Barbie*, the 2023 **live-action** movie. Many other dolls and accessories from the movie were also sold.

Barbie was a big hit. The movie follows a Barbie doll as she learns about the real world. It also features Ken as well as many popular Barbie dolls from over the years. *Barbie* earned more than $1.4 billion. It also made Barbie doll sales quickly rise.

BARBIE MOVIE DOLLS

BARBIE IN PINK GINGHAM DRESS

BARBIE IN INLINE SKATING OUTFIT

PRESIDENT BARBIE

KEN IN DENIM MATCHING SET

BETTER WITH BARBIE

BARBIE DREAM GAP PROJECT ADVERTISEMENT

Mattel and the Barbie brand have many programs to help others. From 2018 to 2019, Mattel gave more than 6,000 play kits to kids in need. Since 2019, the Barbie Dream Gap Project has given $250,000 each year to **charities** that help girls.

PLAYBACK
The Mattel Playback program lets people give unwanted Barbies and other toys back to Mattel. This helps keep plastic waste from harming the earth.

Mattel also created a line of Barbie dolls without hair. It has given 70,000 of the dolls to over 200 different hospitals. Many children being treated at them battle illnesses that can cause hair loss. The dolls can help kids deal with their illness. The Barbie brand plans to keep giving back in the future.

GIVING BACK

6,000 PLAY KITS
GIVEN TO KIDS FROM 2018 TO 2019

$250,000
GIVEN TO CHARITIES THAT HELP GIRLS EACH YEAR SINCE 2019

70,000
BARBIE DOLLS GIVEN TO OVER 200 DIFFERENT HOSPITALS

BARBIE FANS

Many Barbie fans are Barbie collectors. In 2022, a German collector earned the world record for the largest Barbie collection. She owns 18,500 Barbie dolls! Collectors and fans also gather to celebrate Barbie. The National Barbie Doll Collectors **Convention** is a yearly event. Barbie collectors show off their dolls. Fans can also sell dolls, win prizes, and learn Barbie facts.

WORLD'S LARGEST BARBIE COLLECTION

NATIONAL BARBIE DOLL COLLECTORS CONVENTION

WHAT IT IS

A gathering for Barbie collectors

WHEN IT HAPPENS

Once each year

WHERE IT HAPPENS

Around the United States

ACTIVITIES

Meet other collectors, sell and trade Barbie dolls and accessories, and learn about the history of Barbie

Barbie is loved by many. The brand and its dolls have grown and changed. But Barbie remains the world's favorite fashion doll!

GLOSSARY

accessories—items added to something else to make it more useful or attractive

advertisements—public notices that tell people about products, services, or events

animated—produced by the creation of a series of drawings that are shown quickly, one after the other, to give the appearance of movement

brand—a category of products all made by the same company

campaign—a series of planned actions done to achieve certain goals

charities—organizations that help others in need

convention—an event where fans of a subject meet

debuted—was introduced or released for the first time

diverse—made up of people or things that are different from one another

Down syndrome—a condition in which a person is born with an extra chromosome; chromosomes are groups of genes in the body.

founded—started

headquarters—a company's main office

inclusive—including everyone regardless of race, ability, or background

live-action—filmed using real actors

marketed—advertised or promoted

prosthetic—related to human-made devices that replace or improve missing or injured body parts

TO LEARN MORE

AT THE LIBRARY
Abdo, Kenny. *Barbie Franchise*. Edina, Minn.: ABDO, 2024.

Eagan, Cindy. *The Story of Barbie and the Woman Who Created Her*. New York, N.Y.: Random House, 2017.

Sommer, Nathan. *Barbie Dolls*. Minneapolis, Minn.: Bellwether Media, 2022.

ON THE WEB
FACTSURFER

Factsurfer.com gives you a safe, fun way to find more information.

1. Go to www.factsurfer.com.
2. Enter "Barbie" into the search box and click 🔍.
3. Select your book cover to see a list of related content.

INDEX

accessories, 5, 7, 11, 17, 19, 20, 24
advertisements, 9, 16, 26
Barbie (movie), 24, 25
Barbie and the Rockers, 16, 17
Barbie Dream Gap Project, 26
Barbie Dreamhouse, 11, 19
books, 7
brand, 6, 7, 10, 13, 14, 15, 17, 22, 24, 26, 27, 29
careers, 5, 6, 10, 11, 24
charities, 26
collectors, 7, 28
diversity, 13, 15, 19, 22
Dolls of the World, 14
Dream Glow Barbie, 17
early Barbie careers, 10
El Segundo, California, 6, 7
fans, 7, 21, 28
Fashionistas, 22, 23
friends, 12, 13, 17, 18, 25
giving back, 27

Handler, Barbara, 9
Handler, Elliot, 8, 9
Handler, Ruth, 8, 9
Horse Lovin' Barbie, 17
Jewel Girl Barbie, 20
lines, 6, 14, 16, 17, 18, 22, 23, 27
Malibu Barbie, 14
Matson, Harold, 8
Mattel, 6, 8, 9, 10, 11, 15, 16, 17, 18, 19, 22, 26, 27
Mattel Playback program, 26
Mermaid Fantasy Barbie, 20
movies, 5, 7, 16, 21, 24, 25
National Barbie Doll Collectors Convention, 28, 29
sales, 9, 17, 18, 22, 23, 25
Share a Smile Becky, 18, 19
timeline, 19
Totally Hair Barbie, 18
video games, 7, 21

The images in this book are reproduced through the courtesy of: New Africa, front cover (main Barbie); Michelle VP, front cover (*Barbie* movie); NeydtStock, front cover (accessories, Barbies top left), p. 19 (1988 entry); Adryan Samuel Hutagalung, front cover (B letter); seeshooteatrepeat, front cover (Barbie sports car); Anicka S, front cover (shoes pattern); Leka Talamoni, front cover (Barbie and friends); PREMIO STOCK, front cover (Barbie app); Adam Yee, front cover (Barbie silhouette); Sean P. Aune, pp. 2, 3, 11 (bottom), 23 (Barbie sales graph photos); picture alliance/ Getty Images, pp. 4-5, 17 (Barbie and the Rockers); kewe1936/ ebay, p. 5 (Barbie Dreamplane); kaykhoon, p. 6 (Barbie products); JHVEPhoto, p. 6 (Mattel headquarters); Stefano Chiacchiarini '74, p. 7 (top); Ken Lund/ Wikipedia, p. 7 (bottom); Chris Willson/ Alamy, p. 8 (top); MATT CAMPBELL/ Getty Images, p. 8 (Ruth Handler); JuliaDorian, p. 8 (Barbie expo display); Anadolu/ Getty Images, p. 9 (1959 Barbie); ASSOCIATED PRESS/ AP Newsroom, pp. 9 (Ruth and Elliot Handler), 19 (1997); Frazer Harrison/ Getty Images, p. 10 (fashion designer); Chesnot/ Getty Images, p. 10 (astronaut); Eduardo Parra/ Getty Images, p. 10 (surgeon); Mirrorpix/ Alamy, p. 10 (rock star); Gabe Ginsberg/ Getty Images, p. 11 (Barbie Dreamhouse); This is Barbie World/ ebay, p. 12 (Ken); Cynthia Lizana, p. 12 (Allan, Midge); Ink Drop, p. 12 (Barbie logo background); INTERFOTO / History/ Alamy, p. 13 (top); Eddi Frantz/ fashiondolldreamer/ Instagram, p. 13 (Christie); Vintage_Toys_And_ Treasures/ ebay, pp. 14 (Dolls of the World), 16 (Barbie board game), 17 (Horse Lovin' Barbie), 19 (Barbie for President); Chicago Tribune/ Getty Images, p. 14 (Mailbu line); Mel Melcon/ Getty Images, p. 15; DatBot/ Wikipedia, p. 16 (bottom); Betsy Rathburn, p. 18 (top); Yvonne Hemsey/ Getty Images, p. 18 (Totally Hair Barbie); Bill Greenblatt/ Newscom, p. 18 (Share a Smile Becky); Handout/ Getty Images, p. 19 (1961); Mattel/ Warner Bros./ Wikipedia, p. 19 (2023); Teenage doll/ Alamy, p. 20 (Mermaid Fantasy Barbie); Federico Magonio, p. 21 (top); ArcadeImages/ Alamy, p. 21 (video game); Cinematic Collection/ Alamy, p. 21 (movie); Diane Bondareff/ AP Images, p. 22 (Fashionistas line); dpa/ AP Newsroom, p. 23 (bottom); BFA/ Alamy, p. 24 (*Barbie* movie); mariosgames/ ebay, p. 25 (top let, top right, bottom left); nemo10mt/ ebay, p. 25 (bottom right); Bellwether Media, p. 26; ivanastar, p. 26 (bottom); Igisheva Maria, p. 27 (top); ElenaR, p. 27 (bottom left); 8th.creator, p. 27 (bottom right); INA FASSBENDER/ Getty Images, p. 28; Houston Chronicle/ Hearst Newspapers/ Getty Images, p. 29; Melnikov Dmitriy, p. 31 (top right); Genesistr, p. 31 (veterinarian, mermaid).